double dealing dog

double dealing dog

Last in a Long Line of Fine Canines

d.j. posner

Copyrighted Material

Double Dealing Dog
Last in a Long Line of Fine Canines

Copyright © 2023 by D.J. Posner. All Rights Reserved.

All rights reserved. No part of this book may be reproduced or transmitted in any form or by any means, electronic or mechanical, including photocopying, recording, or by any information storage and retrieval system, without permission in writing from the copyright owner.

This is a work of fiction. Names, characters, places, and incidents either are the product of the author's imagination or are used fictitiously, and any resemblance to any actual persons, living or dead, events, or locales is entirely coincidental.

For permission requests or to order additional copies, contact:

D.J. Posner
www.djposner.com

ISBNs:
978-1-7369399-3-2 (hardcover)
978-1-7369399-4-9 (softcover)
978-1-73693995-6 (eBook)

Library of Congress Control Number: 2023912902

2nd Edition—2023

Printed in the United States of America

Cover and Interior design: 1106 Design

This book is kinda' sorta' based on a true story.
A little bit.

This book is dedicated to dog lovers everywhere.
Dogs come in many shapes and sizes, but I have found
the bigger the dog, the greater the love!
—d.j. posner

"Not everything you write is going to be a masterpiece. Not everything you cook is great, not everything you paint—but you're trying for it. From the moment you put the pen to paper or sit down at the piano, you're trying for it."
—Maya Angelou (1928–2014)

chapter 1

It's a long story, worthy of telling as to how I came to own and love Miss Pearl Bailey, one Two-Timing, Double-Dealing Dog! First, for the sake of narration, it may serve well to introduce myself. My given name is Delilah Jasmine, a tried-and-true southern moniker handed down to me by my parents and grandparents. It's been a difficult name to live with in many ways, but, in other ways, it has afforded me some measure of autonomy. So, to keep the peace and stay reconciled within the family tree, I have accepted the title, and, I hope, have worn the name well. Now, with all that established, let's commence with the story of this hellion canine, a tale that actually begins in the years that led up to Pearl Bailey's arrival—the years when my life was filled with two of the world's best dogs.

Joy filled my life and heart in those days. It was easy to love all things, furry and otherwise, when you were greeted each morning with such unabashed adoration. Coming home to your hearth at day's end and being met with oodles of affection completes one's soul. And that was the way my life progressed until the inevitable took away those lifelines.

Let me start with Misha. Misha was a handsome dude, a lesser-publicized French breed known as *Coton du Tulear*. True to his lineage, he possessed great dignity and swagger. At a little less than twelve pounds, Misha dominated his territory with grace and style. With hair as fine as spun silk in tones of apricot and crème, he captivated every being with whom he came into contact. Sporting warm, golden-brown eyes, he possessed a mischievous smile that was evident right down to the tip of his tail.

Misha came to me in an interesting way. At this point, I probably should introduce The Professor, my husband of great joviality. We have been married for eons, and we are complete opposites, but somehow the synergy has worked for us. Relaxed in our newly empty nest with both of his two children thriving in college, and us basically broke paying tuition, contentment still abounded. The freedom that we both had regained was deep and satisfying. Until . . . until one day, when The Professor came sauntering in with what I thought was the most precious ball of fur I had ever laid eyes on. Misha had the semblance of a stuffed animal, and I remember squealing at the sight. Why had The Professor brought this adorable pup to me? The story that follows was quintessentially my husband.

The Professor, a hard-working, no-nonsense soul, had an appointment with a long-time alum, a vibrant and somewhat questionable Frenchman—a colorful character always involved in schemes and dreams. The Professor described that, during this consultation, the gentleman explained that he, in return for The Professor's astute advice, could offer a pup from an unsanctioned litter, a product of his breeding pair. *"Mon Dieu!"* the man declared to The Professor, "The boy dog found the girl dog when I was not looking, and now I can only give the *bébés* away!" As the story dragged on, I came to realize that this was a done deal. *Oh, my,* I thought. Always quick on my feet, I scrambled to defend my liberation from being a caretaker of adopted beings. I excitedly called out, "I can't have a little dog, Sir; I am a big-dog girl!" He just looked at me with a shrug, a sure indicator that it was a done deal. Thus began my love affair with the world's cutest little dog, our Misha!

Chapter 1

Misha was a steady Capricorn soul. I could always rely on him to amuse me and yet sit quietly beside me when that was what I needed more. He was frisky in his puppy years, his spirited antics lending him a reputation among the neighborhood as being wanted more than the FBI's top ten. "Joggers Beware" applied if their path took them past our house. Interposing upon a runner's tranquility, Misha's staccato bark while running the fence line was certainly alarming at best.

Still, we nestled together just fine as the months zoomed by and our little five-pound mass of fur grew into a handsome, prancing dog—true to his show-quality title, of which he had been stripped when his harlot mother made the decision to take on his pursuing father!

chapter 2

It is a fine feeling to be sitting at your desk with a dog on your feet. There is something so satisfying in that dependence. I have never been without at least one dog in my life. My love affair and the parade of big canine companions began with a stunning German Shepherd that my father acquired as a guardian for my mother and us kids while he went to school at night. We named her Heidi after the wonderful family film of the same name. She was a magnificent beast, fiercely loyal and devoted to our family. She served us all well right into her fifteenth year when, mourning the death of our beloved grandfather, she could no longer endure.

It wasn't long thereafter that Sammy took hold in our family. Sammy was a big black Labrador, full of vim and vigor. He thought my father walked on water, and secretly, so did I. My brother and I were teenagers by the time Sammy came to be king in our household. My much-younger sister played an endless game of catch with Sammy on most any day the sun was shining. We lived on a farm in the rolling hills of Maryland, and to this day, I can still see Sammy running, pink tongue flapping incessantly as Sister Golden Hair threw the ball with all her might. Sammy never ceased to amuse even the stodgiest of folk. He had a heart of gold.

Double Dealing Dog

As my brother and I entered college, our lives began to resonate with our respective passions and pursuits, while Sammy was still chasing after things large and small. A very sad and sobering hour it was when I got the call that Sammy had chased his last quest. A truck hauling corn just simply didn't see the big black dog as the evening fell away to darkness. Just like that, Sammy was gone.

Baby sister, at home on the family farm with parents and Grammie all to herself, had a parade of little dogs. There were Maggie and Muffin, and Grammie had Sandy—all fine Terriers, but for me—well, I was a big-dog girl! And once I had my "studies" behind me and became a self-supporting member of society, I immediately sought out a big dog to call my very own.

First in line was Charlie. I acquired Charlie, a husky golden mix of Beagle, Labrador, and something else I could never put my finger on. I like to think that I adopted Charlie, but the truth is he found and adopted me. It was an easy acquisition. My friend was moving

Chapter 2

into a no-pet apartment and needed a home for Charlie. I jumped at the chance. We were fine friends, that big golden dog and me. We went everywhere together. If Charlie wasn't welcome, I wouldn't go. I couldn't get enough of the goofy antics this boy demonstrated on a regular basis. Perhaps the most prevalent memory I have of my Charlie Brown centers around a day I spent in Old Oxford. You see, my father had taken to sailing during that era, and, on one fine summer day, with a stiff breeze blowing from the west, Dad set sail on his beloved yawl, *The Morning Star*, with all the family on-board. Since I was invited, so was Charlie.

At the helm, Dad came-about rounding Basie Point. With the wind at our backs and joy in our hearts, we all gasped at the sight of Charlie as he cocked his leg and piddled on Dad's pants. I guess to this day I am thankful that my father was such a dog lover. Otherwise, I may have found myself and my dog afloat in the Choptank River!

chapter 3

I come from a long line of musicians. My formative years were filled with live music every weekend without ever having to leave my living room. Granddaddy was a picker. He had a fine old arch-top maple jazz guitar made personally for him by master luthier John D'Angelico. Mama played the uke and there was singing, a whole choir of voices that to a youngster sounded like angels. Daddy had bongos and kept the beat. Great Granddaddy, a graduate of the New England Conservatory of Music, was a legendary composer and military band leader of notoriety. A quick and nimble man, he would jump to the keys, stroking them like a folded fan. Mine was a wonderful upbringing.

One day my father walked in followed by three very winded fellows hefting a rosewood Steinway & Sons console piano. This was my father's gift to me. The expectations were high, but I was completely immersed in the confidence that this extraordinary gift inspired. I was eight years old.

I rose to the occasion and have kept music alive in my life ever since. I think Dad would be proud of me today, knowing that I have never let music leave my life. To this day, I compose songs in my head and in my heart, guided by a lilting melody and spurred on by lyrics that roll through my brain. I tell you this not to digress but to give you a clear and concise understanding of the path that life has guided me along.

I wandered during my early adult years. I had music ringing in my ears, and I followed it from town to town, seeking and searching. Yet it was always the profound love of a big dog that brought me home. It's funny how dogs love music. Every pooch that walked my life's path with me would sit quietly while I made music, some of it good, some of it rambling as I tried to find my way through the complicated chorus of life and love.

My wandering eventually prevented me from taking Charlie with me. I was headed to the Rockies and really didn't know what I'd find. Charlie was grateful to be returned to his original owner, who was by now back running his family farm in Mount Airy. Charlie's bones were growing old and achy, and my bones were growing itchy to follow a new direction.

I wasn't in Colorado long before I met a wandering lead guitar-playing cowboy. Born on April Fool's Day, he mesmerized me with his exquisite fingerings along a fret board. But what really captivated me was his big black Lab, Miss Tailpipe.

chapter 4

Tailpipe stole my heart the instant we met. Who can resist a regal dame? She was refined—if one could describe a dog in this manner. I loved every inch of her. We became fast friends. There was no looking back. Having become a lyrical contributor to the beautiful original music being performed and thereby flying on the coattail of stardom, I allowed my quiet self to essentially reside in the wings. I felt that, although I was fifty feet from the spotlight, I was on a certain pathway toward success. We would arrive in each town, a dazzling trio including Tailpipe, each of us making a handsome entrance. Audiences would be carried away by the unique sound of the music we made.

I watched Tailpipe as she would quietly teach other canines who she met in our travels. Her innate manners rubbed off on even the most wretchedly mannered pup. I learned from her sense of domesticity and allowed it to formulate my own approach to life's challenges. I became a wife. I left my concern of self behind and became a caregiver. The boys in the band always turned to me. I carried a "magic bag of tricks," an enormous carpetbag with everything and anything one might need. I cooked for the tour. I sewed torn jeans and served as universal confidante. I wrote beautiful songs, sung by beautiful men. I was content, and Tailpipe was always at my side. It was a great family, two thousand miles from the one I'd left behind.

As the months gave way to years, life evolved into a more domestic mode. Tailpipe was six when she came into my life. She aged gracefully as her pace slowed, and I, anxious to grow our family, found myself elatedly pregnant. What joy to feel the first flutter of knowing that a precious life will enter your world and complete the picture. Tailpipe was at my feet the day I pulled the pregnancy kit stick from the well and discovered its truth. A knowing look passed between us, and I swear to this day, she knew what was to come.

Joy spread throughout our camp, the elation deep. Tailpipe and I set about nesting, the two females in the band. The band settled in Boulder, Colorado, where the music scene was rich. We connected and made big waves of beautiful original music. Life was good . . . until the day when it wasn't. That was the day when the new life inside me expelled itself just weeks into what seemed the perfect moment in time. I was inconsolable. Tailpipe was the one being who nurtured me back from my abyss. She never left my side in the weeks that followed. She allowed me my sadness, and, when she saw me slipping deep into depression, she nudged me to walk in the glorious foothills of Boulder's Flatirons. The healing that finally came was a direct result of this fine and stable mother dog. From the beginning, she shared with me her rightful and established position in this clan.

We walked together every day, we dined together every night, and we inspired greatness in the men we served. We were a team. I will always be grateful for the supportive and unconditional love this magnificent dog gave me throughout her life. A twisted intestine and an acute attack of pancreatitis was what finally took Tailpipe from this earth. Her departure was too soon. She was nine years old. Her quirky name came from her gray snout, apparent at even

Chapter 4

a young age, I was told. Beneath a gunmetal December sky, as a light snow fell, we laid her to rest along a trail that she and I had always walked up in Left Hand Canyon. I will never forget her generous spirit, her loving nature, and her innate ability to heal even the deepest loss.

chapter 5

At this point I should probably explain that all these fine canines led up to my ownership of a Two-Timing, Double-Dealing Dog. It is probably the profound love and acceptance of the canine spirit that I have allowed into my life that has colored my perception. After all, if you have walked with the world's greatest spirits, you must be keen in recognizing the world's worst, right? And not wanting to keep you in suspense, but wanting you to be fully informed, I will continue with the promise that we will get to Miss Pearl Bailey, the double-dealer herself.

One equinox after another fell away, and things began to change. The world was changing, too; boys were coming home from war, and the nation's musical pulse turned to disco. The Age of Aquarius was forming a new world mindset. My maturing soul gained new consciousness as I faced one of life's most profound crises. My lovely cowboy husband, exhausted at the end of a rehearsal, fell asleep behind the wheel coming home. He took with him a beautiful young violinist, a recent graduate of Dartmouth, who was just along for the ride. Angels delivered me the message that his ascent was without hesitation, as my descent into an empty darkness pounded away at my faith and devotion. Shuttered from time and tide, and burying myself in the quiet mindset of reading books, I so sought solitude.

It was not long after—too soon, some said—but I paid them no mind, that a savior appeared. I had heard of this finely educated pianist; his remarkable reputation had been built on skills finely honed; the applause in his life seemed endless. Yet from me, he would not take "No" for an answer. Patiently, he drew me from my self-imposed cocoon and peeled away the painful layers of anguish. With each optimistic note he played, I could no longer wallow. He would cajole me with the music of my childhood, the songs my parents and grandparents played. And more than that, he loved the genre. We were alike. It was a reincarnation, a re-embodiment of a soul that I had somehow known before yet had just met. We married. And present at the nuptials was his magnificent dog named Dolce.

In Italian nomenclature, the musical dynamic term *dolce* is an indication to play in a tender, adoring manner, to play sweetly with a light touch. Our Dolce was the epitome of a sweet and gentle overture. Never a bit of trouble, he would sit quietly, and wherever you would be, he would be beside you. His bark was so infrequent, I often thought something was wrong.

My Pianist traveled extensively—music was his mistress. I was content to remain behind with his big dog to govern my world. I found a job that suited my talents, I made new friends, and I waited. Always returning, my dear man would drag himself in after weeks on the road to find his hearth warmly stoked with a wood fire crackling and a snoring dog sleeping peacefully nearby. I smiled a lot in those days, but I was essentially an island. My partner's greatness was such that I allowed it to consume the space that remained in his wake. It was enough. But as anyone who has held the place of a stanchion in the shadow of another's prominence knows, that, within the magnitude of space that remains inert while the vortex of chaos swirls around you, you begin to lose your footing and any sense of self along with

Chapter 5

it. I longed for home. I missed my family. I spent much of my time alone, and I was lonely.

My sturdy boy, Dolce, delivered me from my doldrums on most days. It was in the need to take care of him that I found solace. He was a quiet soul, and, although our dependence on each other was evident and fulfilling, the quiet enjoyment was not enough to span the distance of my yearning. Although my love for this gentle boy was deep, his quiet soul, it seemed, was not enough to fill the emptiness that my heart had settled upon. That was something new for me. I had always maintained that the unconditional love of a great dog was more than enough to sustain any vacant space.

On a break from his grueling road schedule, my partner and I took a long walk one blissful Colorado evening, with Dolce in the lead. Our talks encompassed deep subjects as I desperately attempted to convey my heart's restlessness. As Dolce sniffed every scent along the way, it seemed we had covered acres of ground as we trudged along, lost in intense and immense conversation. As we rounded the corner at Big Birch path, Dolce simply vanished into the deep, inky dark of the mountain night. I kid you not when I tell you this; our Dolce simply and entirely vanished—he was nowhere to be found. This sure-footed shepherd dog, with innate abilities intrinsic to his breed, had been in the lead during the entire trek. Our discussion certainly was not distracting enough to have prevented us from knowing his whereabouts. That was it. Gone. And we were never to know how or why.

Our global search continued for weeks on end yielding nary a clue. Then the time came when my Pianist husband had to return to his scheduled performances and demanding crowds, and so he left. And now I was really alone. Three long months passed before my mate returned to the hearth. Upon his re-entering the threshold, he found a wife who had begun to break. The loss of our big dog and the resounding solitude of a soulless, empty house began to take their toll. It wasn't long after these feelings had surfaced that life threw me a real curveball.

Chapter 5

The phone rang out in a shrill one evening when my Pianist was home, having just concluded his latest tour. On the other line was my beautiful mother delivering the news no one wants to hear. My father had cancer. It was bad. A glance passed between the two of us, each clutching separate receivers, and it was as if no words needed to be spoken. We were heading back to the East Coast. After all these years, I was going home.

chapter 6

The weeks of planning that ensued in order to make this move happen went by like a whirlwind. There were agents to contact, schedules to cancel, landlord matters to settle, packing, and more packing to be done. All the while, I was elated. Even with the onset of my mother's devastating news, I felt as if my life had somehow returned. It was as if I were moving forward in a direction that had purpose.

Just days before the scheduled departure date, a new soul came into our lives. Enter Ulysses. At the farmer's market one beautiful mountain Spring morning, I strolled past the booth of my friend selling her organic vegetables. We were in a conversation, and I was telling her about my eastern-bound plans; out of the corner of my eye, I spied an English Sheepdog sporting a yellow vest that simply said, "Adopt Me." My heart skipped a beat, and I tell you, I felt as if a lightning bolt had surged up my spine. I concluded business with my friend and left to seek out my husband to continue with our day. He had planned a picnic for us up in Chautauqua Park, in the splendid foothills of Boulder. It was to be a *"kind of"* farewell to the Rocky Mountain state that I came to love so much.

As we climbed the hill to a bucolic spot overlooking our adopted town, the second lightning bolt hit. My husband turned to me and said, "I saw this beautiful shaggy dog at the Market, and I swear he looked right at me as if to say, *I'm available to go with you; I have no other plans*. Again, it was one of those "strike-me-down" moments in which you can sense the direction that you will take. Without hesitation. There wasn't a lot of discussion to this topic; it just came to be.

When our caravan departed down the Peak-to-Peak Highway on our way to Interstate 70 East, safely ensconced on the bench seat in back was the goofiest dog I had ever known!

chapter 7

We rolled in to my parents' home on the Eastern Shore of Maryland on a Thursday morning in May, just days before Mother's Day. I cannot begin to describe the elation in my mother's voice and body language. There I was, old carpetbag in hand, the prodigal one, returning home like cavalry on a rescue mission. Anticipating a settling-in period, I came to realize that this was not to happen. A performance was scheduled for the very next night. That is how fast the spin is in the world of professional music. The announcement of husband's relocation to the Washington, DC, area created a buzz of grand importance. And so it was, the weekend that succeeded our arrival found him immediately performing in Georgetown's premier jazz club of the day. And so began the rhythm and timbre of a new chapter.

chapter 8

There was much to do to face this gargantuan cancer that had silently and balefully taken up residency in the cells of my very special father. The man who could do anything—you name it, he could and would do it. I settled into life back home on the farm, pitching in and being a daily presence within the hallowed halls that was my familial domicile.

If Daddy's beloved boat needed tending to—"No worry, Dad. We'll go. I'll take ya'." If consultation with a doctor was needed, I was there, trudging along. Mama was a hero, her strength and courage borne right up front like a crested metal breastplate. I struggled. I snuggled at night with my goofy dog, Ulysses, because, when I was in that place, there was no sadness, no overwhelming life event to ruthlessly change everything.

Our new home was ready weeks after we arrived. Agents or managers took care of all that. They were kind to me, though. Our new estate was within pitching distance to my family and Grammie. Ulysses and I kept up with the tasks at hand. His goofiness kept me from feeling the deep sadness pervading my heart. Weeks gave way to months. Some said that *these were months we couldn't borrow on*, but finally the inevitable arrived (some may cringe when I use the word "finally," but if you have ever loved someone who cancer took from this world, you do understand). It was not Dad's first deep fall into a critical and pivotal medical event that took him; it was the second. On a cold December evening, soon after I had returned home from a routine Saturday night at Dad's bedside, I got the call to come back. Our Captain had drawn his last breath.

Life was forever changed that chilly winter evening, yet my memories were a comfort. I furiously wrote, the words spilling onto paper as soon as I could get them out. Daddy's eulogy, his whole funeral tribute, was filled with beautiful music, written, played, and performed by people he loved. Some of the homage brought smiles attributed to a lyric so lilting and sweet. Some brought tears, when the words poured out, poignant and piercing. In all of its grief, my opening farewell hit the mark of the woman my father always knew I could be.

chapter 9

Thankfully, husband's performances were limited during the holidays. At a time of year with so much ancillary entertaining going on, often national talent would lay their schedules back in order to accommodate the holiday events. And so it was that I was not alone during the deeply sad and dark days that followed Dad's passing. Even so, quiet permeated even the deepest reaches of my soul. It wasn't so much the sadness that saturated the air; it was the empty space that remained. The holidays that approached seemed lackluster; the songs that had, in years past, ricocheted around in my brain were now stilled. Even the carols that had always uplifted me as a child no longer stoked the Yule embers in my heart.

One evening, just a week into my mourning and days into the season of Advent, husband walked in carrying a box wrapped in Snoopy Christmas paper. I was dozing as he woke me, saying, "This one can't wait." As he lowered the box, the lid popped open to reveal a nine-week Old English Sheepdog puppy, who I named Chelsea Beatrice.

chapter 10

Now, if you are thinking that owning two Old English Sheepdogs could be the most fun job in the world, you would be right. How could the sadness of my loss linger when unabashed goofy love was all around me? Oh, and to witness their two canine souls falling in love with each other, well now, you guessed it, "I'm a romantic."

Chelsea B and Ulysses were a hoot together. You could not help being elated in their presence. English Sheepdogs are just comical in the way they look. With fur covering their eyes and ears flat to the head, they resemble a panda bear. The conformation of the breed was *lower at the shoulder than at the loin,* giving them a rolling-from-the-rear, bear-like gait. It was hilarity to just watch those two traipse across a room. It's been written that every dog has a gift, which, translated, means that every dog has the ability to give and receive love in a healing manner. Therapy comes in many different forms. And when you are in need of treatment, the cure that comes from the love of a dog is as transforming as it is rehabilitating.

Loving Ulysses and Chelsea consumed the months and years that followed, and my maturing soul let me linger a little longer in the vacuity created in our marriage due to the Pianist's peripatetic globetrotting. The loving gesture from the husband in providing me my comedy team gripped and anchored my flighty soul. Years had passed before I realized I was still at anchor, the lee winds long gone.

chapter 11

Chelsea was six when she took ill; This was interesting, as Ulysses was the older of the two. Although they'd never mated, these two souls were like an old married couple. They were so comfortable with each other it gave you the feeling of a deeply satisfying easy chair.

Bladder issues were to be the demise of this comedienne. It became evident quickly, and when that happens, you know that the end is not going to be an easy one. When we had exhausted everything we could do for her, the disease took hold and took her sweet and cajoling love from my world. Ulysses and I were beside ourselves. We both grieved so; our home felt lifeless. Husband, on the road, again, left a vast emptiness in the hearts of the two souls remaining at his hearth.

I had lost a tremendously comedic *daughter;* Ulysses, on the other hand, had lost his *wife,* his *mate.* The ins and outs of the husband's performance-schedule commitments left Ulysses and me going through the almost-inert motions of trying to survive. Within a year of her passing, Ulysses let go, too. I believe he mourned her so, that following her to the next realm was what felt comfortable to him. Somehow, I understood.

Now what remained was what would I do with my empty heart?

chapter 12

Courage comes from many sources. Grace as well. I began to build on a new strength that I had summoned, a strength gained from and fortified by my beautiful mother, whose keen intelligence and wisdom was to become a constant beacon for me.

My writing and occasional composing took on new depth. Buoyed by exacting resonance, I met the mark that had been evading me in the preceding years. Strong and robust words surged out onto paper, and I let them find their way to the mainstream. A voice, my voice, was reaching out, and, although its audience was limited, it was one that encouraged me to provide more and more. I felt like I was reborn.

Those days and hours spent in honing my craft led to a very important encounter that was to become the final dissection of my loveline. The palm of my hand clearly shows a meandering "loveline" that bifurcates twice, resulting in a three-way path. This ancient prophecy was to become certain by a meeting that was set up by my Pianist, who, by now, spent more time devoted to his audiences—and less time squeezed into my ordinary life as a placated writer. It was a natural progression. There were no acrimonious departures or raised swords; it was a gentle coming-apart spurned on by not only personal growth but by each of our professional demands simply fulfilling their respective objectives.

I was looking for a new editorial direction that would help me raise and expand my voice to a wider audience. A longtime friend of my Pianist was a tenured professor at The American University in Washington, DC. Although I had never met him, The Professor and the Pianist had enjoyed a deep and abiding friendship for many, many years, each having been great fans of the other's life work. Since academia hosted a vast arena of young, bright ideas, my Pianist thought it a grand notion for me to meet his friend in hopes that it could introduce a new infusion of young trained minds to support my growth.

I took the train into the city late one Spring morning. The activity on the campus was exhilarating. It had been years since I felt so light in my steps. I soaked up the sunshine from a perch I found under an old Cherry tree until it was time for my pre-arranged appointment. I watched campus life as it streamed by me and sketched out stories that I believe matched up to the faces of the young people careening around me. Audacious in my prose, I created characters that would develop into either genuinely accomplished or deeply depraved creatures, depending on what I saw in their illuminated, or pensive, faces. With the warmth of the sun kindling my muscles, I fell asleep. I'm not kidding—I fell asleep under the tree while waiting for an appointment with a very busy tenured professor.

It wasn't long past two o'clock, the allotted time of my appointment, that I was gently awakened by a stroke up my arm. I heard my name being called as I opened my eyes to see the kindest face of any person I had ever met. His smile was beatific. And besides that, he was adorable. I detected a faint trace of pipe tobacco on his manicured hands. "Goldilocks," he addressed me, "are you late for something?" I startled the rest of the way awake, stammering something completely

Chapter 12

incoherent, as he gently offered his hand to help me up. It was The Professor. He turned and began his walk back into the building, beckoning me to follow. Welcomed by the cool of the air-conditioned halls, I followed—oh, yes I followed—and that's not just a euphemism. As I entered the quiet inner sanctum of his office, I began to relax. Our conversation, which, incidentally, would continue for the next thirty years, began with a simple, "How may I help?" Hours passed before I realized the Spring afternoon was giving away to dusk. The Professor asked if I would enjoy a meal and the prospect of continued exploration into this new-infant-like attraction of minds. Having left Mother in charge of any domestic responsibilities back on the estate, I agreed. A phone call to advise her went out to the Eastern Shore, and off I went, hot on the heels of my new pied piper, although, at the time, I had no idea of what was to come my way.

chapter 13

The days and weeks that followed were filled with introductions and dates in the city, where I was learning to fill my literary psyche with expanded vision. The Professor introduced me to a wide world that stretched well beyond my privileged, protected sanctum. I listened and reached, and broke free of my corseted expectations, and my writing blossomed as a result. All the while that my mind was awakening, so was my heart. *Oh, my.* This was quite a fix I had placed myself in. All of the late-afternoon conferences fell away into evening meals and endless conversation. Then I would make the long drive back to the estate to find my beautiful mother waiting, never judging but being completely conscious of the changes at hand. It was she who finally held up the mirror to my face wherein I beheld the softness and blush of my easily recognizable transformation. *Oh, my.*

I struggled with my heart's intuition. The time was fast approaching when my Pianist husband was due back at the hearth. Would the physical change that I was experiencing be transparent? It had been a grueling three-month run for him. Returning to home base would mean many management meetings and schedule-building for the next run. It exhausted me to even think about it. I was in a buoyant state, in a place where my lively self reigned magnificent. How would I handle the change in pace, the refocus? *Oh, my*—what a dilemma! I longed and yearned for detachment, but it wasn't in me. The omnipresent *mistress-muse* between my Pianist and me refused to be silenced, and I did nothing to quiet it. It was as important to me as it was to him that *she* be allowed to exist. *She* was ingrained in him, and his talent was something that belonged to the world, not just me alone. I braced.

chapter 14

The first week of my Pianist's return was like an old worn shoe—comfortable and easy. The madness of his professional world slowly crept in like a bandit thief, and by the end of the second week, the endless phone calls and schedule changes had me reeling.

One evening, my Pianist slipped into the conservatory and joined me. I was perched beside the fire, reading. His mood was light and agreeable, so I relaxed. As he opened the bottle of chilled champagne he was holding, he handed me a glass. And with a lingering yet wistful smile, he also handed me my freedom. And that was it. No accusatory hurls, no discordant retorts. I was free to move in the direction that my heart was leading me. For the second time in my life, a courageous man had let me go so that I could soar. The first was my beloved father, who brought me up and never let me down. Who breathed life in me and encouraged all possibilities. My father set me free when it came my time to leave the nest, to reach for the stars in a faraway mountain town. And now, once again, that same courage and grace was applied by this lovely soul who wanted more for me than what he was able to provide.

And so, a new chapter would begin for me. It would be filled with all of the possibilities that I had once dreamt about . . . a family, two children, and the greatest dog who ever lived in life . . . a big, yellow Lab named Kelsey.

chapter 15

And so it was that I became a bride for the third and last time. The Professor's children stood at our sides as our vows were spoken under a *chuppah* laced with wisteria and lilacs. My beautiful mother beamed with the knowledge that fulfillment had finally found me, her prodigal one. The remarkable thing was that the abiding friendship of the Pianist and The Professor continued in perfect stride. It was almost as if there was an innate sense in the Pianist's awareness that foretold the outcome of my introduction to The Professor. I never viewed it any different than a gift, a gracious and selfless gift that allowed me my voice without penance or struggle. I used the gift to its fullest, my grateful soul encouraged to flourish.

Double Dealing Dog

Some were shocked by, and even more snickered at, the synergy of the relationship that endured within the trio. For the ones who did not know the history, there was no marvel. For the ones who did, the ultimate ensemble was finally realized. Even the most stubborn naysayer couldn't deny the grace that was present. Our supporters' warm respect was directly attributed to The Professor's, the Pianist's, and my maturing souls. Besides, the dog LOVED all three of us—and if the dog was gifting and giving love, well, enough said.

Kelsey was an altruistic soul. With lilting head and supportive eyes, she was able to rescue and lift the spirits of everyone she met.

Life, *real* life, abounded in my new family. The kids were breaking down walls and achieving progress like my generation never had. Kelsey was a great nurturer; she herded our extended family in every way possible, even with the Class V heart murmur with which she was born.

Life with a dog is complete. Home is where the dog is. Kelsey was almost human in her devotion. As much as I have loved all the dogs in my life, the love Kelsey returned on any given day was magnanimous and took me to a place in my heart I had never felt before.

With the kids in college and The Professor in lectures, Kelsey sat at my feet or beneath my piano as I wrote. Her presence was constant as I read aloud my emergent prose. As much as I am a *natural* spiritual being, I've always wondered as to how two souls might have possibly communed in earlier times. But it was clear to me that Kelsey's and my souls had walked together in the same roles but on some other astral plane. When I say she was the *best dog that ever lived in life*, it was not an exaggeration. Owning an intelligent dog is a great gift, but owning an intelligent and deeply loving dog is a miracle. I was so thankful that Kelsey had blessed my life.

As years gave way, Autumn came and went with her shod leaves signifying a finale fêted by heavy-handed winter solstices, quiescent

Chapter 15

despite the promise of a reborn Spring. Kelsey, who was so perfect in every way, stopped running one day in her tenth year. This astounding pup, of whom it was said she would not reach her first birthday, had defied all odds by championing through ten full years of life, fostering love with every human she encountered. I laid her to rest on the estate under the shade of an ancient oak. I planted crocus bulbs over her and, when the next Spring arrived, her *chi* delivered a warming array of brilliant color to the land that rambled along the bend of the river she so loved. As heartbroken as I was to lose my best friend, I did not mope or mourn. I rejoiced in grateful joyfulness that I had been able to love to this depth.

chapter 16

Have you ever had a muse? Have you ever *been* one? In classical mythology, a muse (regarded as a noun), is the god or goddess thought to be inspiring to a poet, an artist, a thinker, or the like. Max and Misha were my muses. You remember Misha, the world's cutest little dog? We met him in Chapter 1. But you haven't met Maximus Aurelius, my gladiator dog!

When Kelsey left this Earth, there was a hole in The Professor's and my hearts. It was even shared by the children, both of whom had grown up with her. Grown Daughter and I had seen a flyer on the wall while in the veterinarian's office. The litter of Newfoundland pups was ready for release. Oh, my. Now remember, I am a Big Dog Girl! You recall that was my weak defense against the adoption of Mighty Misha! Well, let me tell you—I found myself meandering down the Shore to the little town of Bozman to a breeder's home, where the warmest ball of black fur wrapped his paws around The Professor's neck. That was all it took. Wow! Now I *really* was a big-dog girl!

chapter 17

Misha never quite took to Max. It was as if he mildly tolerated him. You see, there was no Alpha between Kelsey and Misha. Kelsey's altruistic soul would not allow that. Misha and Kelsey were a natural pair; their devotion to each other was *simpatico*. When Max entered an already-grown male dog's terrain, he dominated—if not immediately, at the very least soon after—due seemingly to his size!

Even though they pretended not to like each other much, they grew to love each other quietly. Max watched out for Misha. Max watched out over us all. If you were in Max's pack, you were watched over. And believe me when I tell you, if you were in Max's pack and something negative came your way, it would have to go through Big Max to get to you.

As the mother of Max, you can well imagine the respect and devotion I received. I was protected. We became inseparable. On the occasion that I had to travel and left the boys with their caretaker, Max would mope and wait until the minute I walked through the door again. And the next minute, it was as if I had never been gone. That is an innate ability that is built into the DNA of a dog. They live in the present moment—nothing else matters. I was his leader, his love, his life. He was mine, faithful and true. I read once that "Dogs come into our lives to teach us about love; they depart to teach us about loss. A new dog never replaces an old dog; it merely expands the heart. If you have loved many dogs, your heart is very big." I know that this is true. For my heart just swelled with no bounds in order to hold all the love I had for Max and Misha, my two furry muses.

chapter 18

I built a sturdy life; contentment was deep. I had my big dog, Maximus, and he had me. And, Misha would be always at my feet on the bed, having been lifted there by me at lights-out. His regal royal rump delicately placed in his rightful throne, Misha, for the next few hours, would be a sleeping King. Life was good.

Months peeled away to years, and, one by one, the trips around the sun started stacking up like a deck of cards. My bones were getting itchy again. I had lost Mother two years before, although it still felt like yesterday. My boys, all three of them, were beginning to show their age. Maturing bones, tired eyes, and fatigued muscles reminded us all that the days on this Earth had become shorter.

I started to examine my place on Earth. Both of my parents had left this world much too early; time was shorter now. I sought a remedy for my itchy bones, and, miraculously, I found it! Warm Florida sunshine.

I began to dream about it. And slowly, like any great plan, I put it into motion. First, a beach house. Not just any beach house—The Professor insisted it must be walking distance to the Gulf. And find it we did!

Double Dealing Dog

Next, a retirement scheme; well now, that would be harder to come by. You see, The Professor was tenured, and in this world, it is not easy to replace the acumen and insight, both of which younger academia was lacking. But I could be persistent.

Slowly the plan began to gel, but there was only one problem. Big Max could barely walk. He made the trip south a couple of times—a champ, really. He found my beach, and, I'm told, loved it as much as I did. But his bones could barely support his giant frame. And then there was the incessant agony, only somewhat silenced by six pain pills a day. As my noble, magnificent boy was weakening, my heart was breaking in the process. I just didn't see it coming. How could I?

chapter 19

On July 22, we celebrated Max's eighth birthday. He was happy, as he always was when his pack was present. But a few short weeks later, his eyes were to tell me that it was his time to go. I moved into the conservatory and began to play. I played every song I knew; I sang along sweetly, words choking up and faltering. Slowly, I heard his footsteps in the hall. He made it to the French doors outside and slid down against the wall. I continued my serenade, its tribute falling down around us like stars. When I finished, I lay on the floor beside him, Misha asleep on top of the sofa, unaware. We made a pact, Big Max and I. He would let me know when he made it to the other side. I would be waiting.

On August 8, I took a punch below the belt. I said goodbye to this most imperial of beasts who'd loved and protected me without reserve, without question. I sobbed the tears of a child, the strength of my womanhood exhausted. There was only thing I could think of to do—escape to the Florida sunshine.

Misha, our healthy 14-year-old, of course, stoically made the trip with us. Although uncertain by the emptiness of the space that Max used to occupy, he was grateful that it was all his own. We all let the sunshine heal us and warm our shoulders, the emptiness slowly attenuating. When we had had our fill, we returned up north to our beloved Eastern Shore to trudge through another academic year and a new slew of freshman minds that needed molding. I returned to my word processor and furiously wrote Max's eulogy, pouring out like torrential rain from a thundercloud.

he made it
(a eulogy for max)

Maximus Aurelius
July 22, 2005—August 8, 2013

I let go the other day. I let my love take a nosedive to the bottom of the tank with your warm brown eyes telling me everything I needed to know. I loved you, beyond all others; your soul gifted to me eight wonderful years ago. That first hug, the paws wrapped around the neck as if you knew that these would be the humans who would care for you, and you them.

How gallant you were in your lifetime. My proud, regal boy, so handsome. How cheerful and joyful you were in your guard, and how fortunate I was that your grace was so consuming and that I was so fulfilled.

Why is it, since the last time I saw you, there has been something beautiful to see in the sky? A rainbow, a cumulus cloud, a wispy blue vastness, something to behold? Why is it that I see beauty every time I look upwards? And why do I feel you here—not like yesterday, when you rose to greet, but beside me, where I can still lean into you and you never waver.

I will never be the same. I will remain forever changed by your elegance. We made a fine family—your brother, whose dependence you never had much use for, misses you; he cried the first week-and-a-half. My Aunt Shirley says, "We will all meet in the end on Rainbow Bridge." I suspect that's true. Meanwhile, my job is not yet complete.

You sent me my message—it was the pact we made before you left. That rainbow causeway, glorious in the yet-unsettled sky, the heart-shaped cloud right beneath it, the following evening . . . My heart soared when I received the message, my peace spreading throughout my veins just to know you made it to the stars and found an astral plane where you can reside both here and there.

Thank you, my friend, for all that you have done for me and all that you will do for me, beginning this new day . . .

chapter 20

If I was forever changed by the passing of Big Max, it was the one-two punch that the fates eventually had in store that would have me undone.

Misha, my *never-miss-a-meal* Misha! The sturdiest of boys, never sick in his lifetime, became listless. At first, I thought the departing of Maximus' soul was affecting him outwardly. After several trips to the veterinarian, a mass was discovered, an inoperable, swift-growing mass. Once again, cancer invaded my world like a robber baron. It wasn't but a couple of weeks that the end came upon us. On September 15, Misha left us; Destination: Rainbow Bridge.

Now, when one does the math, it is staggering that these two tragic events occurred a mere five weeks apart. I was inconsolable, heartbroken, and in despair. The Professor's attempts at raising my spirits were comforting, yet nothing could fill the void in my world. The once-hallowed halls seemed drained of life. Returning to an empty house daily, I moped, and I moped.

Months dissolved to season's end, and, upon The Professor's winter semester break, we headed to the Florida sunshine, where he hoped the warmth would heal my broken heart. Rambling down Interstate 95, I would ruefully glance back at the empty nest in the

Double Dealing Dog

back of the SUV, a painful reminder of the double loss. The Professor made an unexpected right turn toward the Virginia valley, where the Blue Ridge Mountains converge with the Great Smoky range. And that is where Miss Pearl Bailey entered our lives!

hold on to your seats, and don't get up . . .

As promised, here is the tale of Miss Pearl Bailey— that Double-Dealing Dog!

chapter 21

After having had all that male-canine testosterone drained from my days, what I yearned for most was sweet and loving female companionship. Like my Kelsey. I imagined a dainty, classy *femme fatale* who could live up to the name, "Miss Pearl Bailey!" What I met in that glowing Carolina winter afternoon was a rough-and-tumble tomboy. She was a hunting machine from stem to stern, the type that would smoke any form of prey from out of the bush, from shoreline sawgrass or from below the Earth's surface. She would dig down to Hell's Gate and snarl at the devil to open it should she sense any form of worthwhile quarry. The lavender "pearl"-studded collar that I bought as adornment did not suit her in the least. This tempestuous streak was apparent from the very first week. Arriving in Florida after I had proudly prodded her for miles "that we were almost to paradise," she promptly proceeded to dig up an in-bloom Bird of Paradise plant nestled at the entranceway of our front door. Ugh! Patience—she's five months old, remember?

Within days, the path of destruction she left in her wake was pandemic; she pulled up two exquisite miniature-specimen palms flanking the planter boxes in the rear deck area and annihilated

Double Dealing Dog

them to smithereens. Next, she escaped to the neighbors' and dug holes in their perfectly manicured yard. She broke leash and swam 60 yards out into the Gulf of Mexico, leaving me alone on shore to wonder if she could really swim. If there was a dog Olympiad, this dog could have medaled in about five events.

Chapter 21

Oh, and she had no use for female companionship. At this stage of my life, I had hoped for a sweet girl-dog who would listen up and go with me everywhere. I longed for a dog-spirit that would attach itself to me; what I got was a man-crazy, demon dog, into everything that she shouldn't and nothing that she should. My peaceful, temperate days were turned into a nightmarish frenzy, every waking hour consumed with the prevention of destruction! She had the uncanny ability to move North, South, East, and West all at the same time. The Professor took to calling her a *blvald (pron.* buh-vohl), Yiddish for *by force*! She was a force of nature. It can be said that she certainly possessed a bounty of exuberance for life! And try as I may, I was unable to break her of it!

And then there was that face. Oh—such beauty should be outlawed. The most fetching, golden-brown eyes were accentuated by thick, long, cream-colored lashes. That face should have come with a remedy. She was a heartbreaker.

chapter 22

The winter break flew by, and, before we knew it, we were headed back to the Eastern Shore to begin another semester. I missed the sunshine before its warmth had barely left my shoulders. Encouraged that the acres of sacred, hallowed grounds of the estate would render some sense into this crazy dog, we returned with hopeful hearts. Yet, back in residence, the rhythm never quite took hold. Pearl Bailey's tempo never descended below *allegro*—fast and lively! And mine, well, I was still on Florida time, which is purposefully slow. Plus, after the recent years caring for my geriatric boy dogs, I was completely unglued running after this maniac. I spoke sweetly to her. I gave her the evil eye and issued warnings, all to no avail. Pearl Bailey was incorrigible. Once all my hopes dashed of rehabilitating her, I enrolled her in obedience school. Now might be a good time to disclose some facts.

The normally penny-wise Professor had dropped a small fortune on this diva as she had already graduated *magna cum laude* from Canine College. Her behavior while at the breeder's ranch was nothing but exemplary. Since the predicament was that she simply never viewed me as her master, I thought a "refresher" was in order.

Pearl Bailey excelled in class. She walked politely, sat and listened without distraction, and demonstrated her cuteness by assuming her favorite position of lying on her back with all four paws in the air, a pose she would hold for an hour if left alone. Of course, she delighted the other dog owners and was held in esteem by the instructors, all of the male persuasion. With The Professor or any of his many friends, she was a delight, a dedicated flirt, entertaining them with unabashed cuteness along with her rough-and-tumble aggression at tug-of-war. But without a male audience to electrify, she would revert to her wild side, confounding me and exhausting my patience.

The front yard of the estate was a full acre of gently rolling green lawn. Picturesque in its perfection, the lawn's upkeep was my prideful duty. Miss Bailey, to whom mere running water hearkened as live prey, soon discovered the subterranean irrigation system and had a hankering for it. Hundreds of feet of soaker hose were dug up and exposed and then annihilated beyond recognition. I fixed it. She did it again. I fixed it. She gloated and ran from my shouting figure as I wielded the punctured hose in hand. This exercise was to be repeated two more times before I ran out of patience—and ran out of budget in fixing it. Having turned the ground drip zone off permanently, I took to watering both the grass as well as the ancient boxwoods by hand.

Her next victims were the prized oriental rugs collected over many years that graced the main house. The regal Pearl Bailey felt they were much more attractive with holes chewed in each corner. The destruction was neatly uniform—I'll give her that. In each corner, she had chewed a hole. I kid you not—every corner of every rug throughout the rooms had holes chewed in them. That's four holes per rug. For God's sake, did she think there was a thrush hiding in the fabric? It looked as if some alien being had descended, discharging a four-prong laser at the floor coverings.

Yet, innocence pervaded her persona, and I was left in a quandary as to how to alleviate her dual personality and regain some semblance of order to my genteel life.

Chapter 22

chapter 23

Spring gave way to Summer, and then came those languid days on the Eastern Shore of Maryland which are nothing less than glorious. Sailboats dot the Chesapeake Bay like a mélange of bobbing kite tails. Blossoms begin to appear everywhere—from the sweet faces of the early pansies to the brush plumes of the Pampas grasses. Uncommonly beguiling and exquisite in every direction you look, this little corner of the Earth has been deemed "The Land of Gentle Living."

In keeping with the estate schedule, we opened the pool and the spa for our guests. Believing that Pearl Bailey would take no interest in either the pool or the spa proved to be a very misguided way of thinking. Day One had her prowling around its perimeter, gracefully prancing across the spillway that separated the two pool areas. After an hour or so of repeated exploration in this manner, a splash of great volume was heard and, *voila*, there she was, swimming perfect laps beside The Professor, himself chuckling between breaths. The *splash*—oh, the splash. That is the big attraction. Being waterfowl hunters and huntresses, these dogs are ready even in the womb for anything that makes water either move or create the slightest of sounds. Splash translates to "grouse down," and then the mode switches to search-and-destroy!

Double Dealing Dog

I was not so amused contemplating this new obsession of hers, which I knew was to become daily regimen. Right I was. Every day thereafter, it was the same routine. Upon waking and with morning coffee in hand, I would let Pearl Bailey out to give her an opportunity to complete her morning toiletry. Within minutes of her release, the splash was heard, and there she was, swimming laps without strain. She would *not* stay out of the pool. That factoid equates to a constantly wet dog—a soaking, sopping, smelly wet dog traipsing around, everywhere and for every waking hour. After each hourly swim, she would dart up the swim steps, prance over to the manicured mulched flower beds and proceed to roll in that dirty concoction until she was no longer recognizable. Next, she would run like the wind throughout the grounds to "air dry" her pelt. When the warmth settled around her, back into the pool she would dive and begin the laps again. This routine never deviated—I kid you not. It would be repeated hour after hour after hour. Swim, Roll, Run, Swim. Over and over again.

The only way to get her to stop was to put her in the house (but you'd have to catch her first). My normal high energy and positive spirit were challenged beyond measure. I instituted all kinds of methods to prevent the occurrence of this daily escapade. I tried using a leash and taking her out through the front door—this was not successful, owing to the *Squirrel du Soleil* act that those wild critters would perform in the ancient oaks lining the drive. This bushy-tailed, flying menagerie tantalized Miss Maniac, causing her to attempt to dislocate my arm from its socket. After several mornings of this painful pursuit, I tried exiting from the carriage-house side of the property, which led to the pond. I wryly thought a jaunt around the pond would be calming. *Wrong.* The pond's teeming amphibian life produced glee in this enthusiastic pup. This, in turn, elicited panic in me as a result of my efforts to halt her attempts into the murky, scummy waters. Again, the *splash* is the trigger. Exhausted from all

Chapter 23

the various methods that I had applied in keeping her in check, I finally acquiesced to her hourly pool activity. At least chlorine smells better than pond scum.

It wasn't too long after I gave in to her watery whims, maybe a month or so, that she changed her routine. She added an unwilling collaborator. She would smoke out a baby frog from the sawgrass that surrounded the pool deck, proceed to nudge it into the pool, advance to the deep end, dive in after it, and chase it back and forth, until it tired out, whereupon she would gulp it down! I was horrified the first time I witnessed this carnage. And, sad to say, I got used to this stalking by just walking away, shaking my head.

chapter 24

Over the succeeding months, Pearl Bailey began to mature, in calendar days only, but her antics never wavered. My plans to let the Florida sunshine light my path was slowing coming into focus. As hard as it was to move from the Eastern Shore and to let my charmed life slip away to a life yet uncharted, my itchy bones were ready. Parting with the estate that had graced my days for twenty or so years took great resolve and steadfast determination. The Professor, who analyzed everything, took the position that this decision was one to take on pensively. He had come to love the grounds as much as I had. We took to calling him *padrón*, as he could be frequently found walking the domain's perimeter, pipe smoke wafting up across the sightline.

To make this enormous leap, I turned to my cousin, who I also consider a trusted friend. Confident that his wisdom would shed light on the best approach to shifting our sands, I sought answers. Cousin was also in a low place, and I had been keeping him under my watchful eye for several months. You see, his beloved bride had left this Earthly plane too soon. She was his bride for forty-plus years, raising his children and his spirits, and infusing sparkle into every day of his life. And now, life looked lackluster as he trudged along existentially while bouncing from one land-development project to another.

Committed to finding the best deal for me, Cousin devoted much of his time to the research and land studies necessary to liquidate the estate and its assets. Because this pursuit had him present at the estate almost daily, Miss Bailey set her cap for ownership of his affection. Yes, she was hell-bent on claiming him as *her man*! It was the strangest thing.

We come to admire different people for different reasons. As we continue down our pathway, we love or laugh or rely on the judgment and amusement of each other to light our way. We keep close those spirits which complete and complement our own nature. This is the way it was with Cousin. Though a decade apart in age, our spirits just communed. He, too, had a deep admiration for animals. It was that which sparked his first attraction to his bride, for there was not an animal on this green Earth who would not sidle up to his sweet wife like a magnet. I admire this in a person—if an animal is notably fascinated with a human spirit, I think that speaks volumes on how a person stands in his or her own skin.

Pearl Bailey was incorrigible in her flirtation with Cousin. When he would drop by the house, upon his departure, she would tear after him and jump into his car. If I had her out with me on an errand, and we swung by his house, she'd be out the door or window as fast as a lightning streak! She was determined to win him, and this left me feeling a little lonely. It was like Cousin had become her very own chattel, and she was not going to take *"No"* for an answer. Oh, what to do with her? And, hey, Pearl Bailey . . . what am I—chopped liver?

I feared that giving Miss Bailey the latitude to pursue her attachment would eventually lead to alienation. What I was looking for, and was in need of, was a devotee of my own. And though her friendship gave me a fondness, it lacked the deeply regarded affection that I had known with my boys and Kelsey. It left me sad.

chapter 25

Cousin's endless land development swept him into and out of our daily routines. When I tell you my household was alive with electricity when Pearl Bailey and Cousin were together, it was like a reunion each time.

Life progressed in rapid succession, the weeks giving away to months in transitioning my life's work into a new normal. My pursuit kept me on track, and Pearl Bailey remained at my side, albeit a subdued soul. I felt like I was crippling a spirit. She brooded whenever it was just the two of us, which was frequent, as The Professor was entrenched in concluding his teachings. Having spent four decades in the molding of young minds, it was difficult for him to let go of his appointment and clasp the tenet that I was embracing.

Yet, the pieces were coming together, and I could feel change in the air. Professor assured me he was committed to this move. Like the Jimmy Buffett song, we sought a tropical latitude giving way to a tropical attitude. It was high time we let our hair down. The rush and race of the metropolitan Washington area was maddening and frantic. The frequent trips we took to "our" island made all the city strains melt away.

Finally, the day arrived when the caravan would depart for southern shores. The moving van pulled out hours ahead of us as we tended to last-minute details. The estate had been purchased by a lovely young family with political ties to the Eastern Shore. I felt so blessed to know that the significance of the property would live on, growing rich and developing vigorously with the spirits of idealistic youth.

Our SUV was packed comfortably, and we were ready to hit the open road, but where was Pearl Bailey? She had been in sight the entire time the moving van was being loaded, insinuating herself more than once up the ramp of the 26-foot truck! But now that our final departure was upon us, she was nowhere to be found. I fumed. I searched and called, and fumed some more. Professor called the neighbors in the event she had made her way off the estate and over to one of the other properties, and, of course, this was to no avail. Finally, after hours of searching, I returned to the front stoop. There, as if she were an infantry warrior who had just crawled on her belly across no-man's land, she sat covered in mud and stinking to high heaven. This dog was going to be the absolute death of me!

chapter 26

We arrived on the Key on an unusually temperate summer day. Although the reputation of Florida's summer months conceptualizes oppressive heat and humidity, Floridians never protest. I loved that about the natives, and it was definitely something I intended to emulate.

Pearl Bailey, having made many trips to our island abode, loved it, too. Why? you might ask. The allure was all about the lizards. And let me tell you, in the summer months on the Suncoast of Florida, those tropical reptiles enjoy their freedom most everywhere you look. This was nirvana to Miss Bailey. Her main pursuit in life was to smoke out the gecko population and eradicate it from the face of the Earth. The first rapture was in the pursuit—stalking, sporting, foraging, and turning everything inside out and outside in. Further glee came with the capture. Not one to settle with annihilation and also being a huntress of great pride, she would proceed in swallowing her prey in one gulp. Of course, I was beyond horrified.

Our island home was situated on a quiet, lazy lane surrounded by an abundance of flora, including the Royal Palms that grace the entrance of the grounds. Just three hundred steps to the most glorious beach, its allure pulling us daily to the sparkling Gulf of Mexico waters.

Double Dealing Dog

The Key we chose is known for its fine, soft, white quartz sand. Most other beaches are made mostly of coral, but Siesta Key's sand is 99% quartz crushed into a pure white fine powder. Geological studies by such discerning universities as Harvard discovered that, through the millennia, quartz from the northern Appalachian chain flowed down surface, as well as subterranean rivers, until the mixture was eventually deposited into the Gulf of Mexico and subsequently onto the shores of Florida's Gulf barrier islands. Because the grains of "sand" are so fine, this process was eons in the making. Quartz sand does not hold the heat of the sun like coral sand does. On the Maryland seashore, it was always a run to the beach blanket so that you didn't burn the soles of your feet. Here, on the baby-powder sands of the Key, it is a common practice of most locals to deposit their flip-flops at the edge of the beach, not needing them until their return to the parking area.

Once we settled our life into this incredible part of the world, The Professor went about setting up a virtual lecture hall. Retirement, for this tenured educator, did not come easily. The years of mentoring and advising a classroom of inquiring minds simply would not fall away. Apparently, his pursuit needed to continue into a world of online teaching. He became entrenched in developing the courses he would

Chapter 26

continue to teach. I didn't totally mind the distraction of the process. I had set about filling my hours with becoming indoctrinated into the local scene. I made new friends with some of the most fascinating people, whose past lives were rich with worldly travel and education; they enjoyed coming to know me, and I them!

I would walk to the beach each and every day to connect with friends and communicate with the natural systems of the cosmos. I could not take Pearl Bailey on these jaunts because she was such a nuisance to the other beach dwellers. She was a maniac both on- and off-leash while in the proximity of any body of water and, simply put, I could not control her. If it was genetically possible to morph the Flying Wallendas, the Road Runner cartoon character, and Jerry Lewis into one being, then you would have Pearl Bailey at her calmest moments!

So the world of Little Beach became mine alone to treasure and commune. I imparted my secrets to the breeze and let my prayers float off to my angel's ears.

The Professor, too, became a beach bum. His sun-kissed skin turned a tawny brown. and the extra pounds packed on from city living fell away, returning his physique to that of his younger self. One day we combed the beach and found a large shark's tooth. The Professor wrapped wire around it and strung it from a cord. This was to become the only jewelry I ever saw The Professor wear. Miraculous. Our hair became more silver from the sunshine, and the backs of our necks were tickled by the shaggy length of our unfettered tresses. Our new calm was easily apparent, but Pearl Bailey's was not. She was not happy being alone while we took our few hours on the beach each day. At the estate, there were always people around to entertain her or amuse her. Here, living on island time, The Professor and I were Pearl Bailey's only distraction, and we had become staid and introspective, simply not acceptable to her mantra for what life should be all about!

Double Dealing Dog

In light of her boredom, a new notion was to take hold of Miss Bailey. She discovered the chickens across the lane. Our neighbor, whose yard was a tropical-paradise jungle befitting a faraway Caribbean island, raised free-range chickens and shared the eggs with all of us neighbors. Can you imagine how delightful it is to be presented each morning with a basket of fresh eggs? It was the most heavenly treat! Well, imagine my horror when Miss Bailey figured out an escape route over to the range, gunning for barnyard fowl. The cacophony of chickens squawking and flying at low altitude with a hound speeding behind in flurried fury was something I never wanted to encounter. Thank God she never caught one, and thank goodness my neighbor was an animal lover and tolerated this abhorrent conduct. I am happy to report that her behavior did not deter my steady supply of eggs. At least not immediately.

chapter 27

Months fell away, eventually marking our first year of retirement. Our Pearl Bailey was still bored with her lot in life, and so it was that I decided that she needed companionship. Now, was this notion for me, or was it for Pearl Bailey? After all, in the process of adopting Miss Bailey, I had made it clear that I yearned for a loving female canine to embrace me and return the devotion. As you know from reading this story, this is not the result I achieved! Perhaps a smaller furry pup, like my Misha, would fit the bill and eventually rouse Pearl Bailey's maternal instincts. It would also provide me with a cuddle love all my own.

I began my search for a pup in earnest during the autumn. My aim was to concentrate on possible pups after a summer of breeding. The pursuit was tugging at my heart. Male or female? White or tri-color? Pedigreed or mixed breed? All the new *designer* breeds on the market presented many more choices. It was overwhelming. I made lists. I spoke with breeders and veterinarians. I combed the online sites and compared. Where was the girl who lived spiritually, who let the mystic and metaphysical guide the process? I had become obsessed! And interestingly enough, nothing ever gelled.

All I knew was that I wanted a small dog. Yes, a small dog. I know, I'm a Big Dog girl. But, hey—I'm also a sensible girl, and, with each passing birthday, I become more and more so. My notion of a furry, little, dainty-type, maybe a missy I could name Ella Fitzgerald (after all, shouldn't I have two dogs named after two jazz greats?), was constantly hitting a stone wall. There was always some kind of energy that reined the idea in or put up a blockade. Progress was not to be realized. Meanwhile, here's Old Miss Mopey Pants giving me the hairy eyeball.

I came to realize that regimen was what Pearl Bailey abhorred. I have been accused of being an ethereal thinker with my head in the clouds often, but I do vibe to routine. I function well with it. I would get up the same time each day and take Miss Bailey on a morning walk; come home and have coffee and breakfast, and feed the girl; work in the office or at housework for a few hours, and walk Miss Bailey for walk number two; head to the beach for a few hours, come back, and walk her a third time; finally, I ended my day with tending to dinner, feeding the girl, and finally walking her again before bed. Boring? Maybe. But consider this . . . during all of the in-between time, Miss Bailey was at liberty to roam free in an expansive-yet-contained, landscaped paradise in order to chase lizards to her heart's content or decimate palm fronds simply because they had fallen into her immediate vicinity. Now, maybe I'm wrong, but, by my standards, I thought I was providing a damn good childhood for this vixen. I guess my only crime was that I was not born a man.

chapter 28

As the seasons changed not once but twice, I continued my search for Pearl Bailey's companion canine. Even though I was not having much luck, I just knew that the right dog soul would reveal itself. Meanwhile, daily routines were being followed, and our Florida home never seemed to lack activity, but not the kind of activity that would be of any use to Pearl Bailey.

As the months of calendar pages turned, spring season arrived, and the crowds that flocked to our southern climate began to thin out. With most of the snowbirds gone back to roost on the northern shores from whence they came, a quiet calm seemed to descend upon our shore. This is when I discovered something that would be both a blessing and a curse to Pearl Bailey's boredom. A Dog Beach! Yes, a glorious dog beach, where canine hearts could soar. An off-leash, run-about, frolic-filled beach with other like-minded canine souls. Oh, my, I can't even put into words the delight and rapture in Miss Bailey's heart the first time I took her there. When I tell you that a new sense of zeal was instilled down deep into the psyche of Pearl Bailey, it is an understatement of great magnitude.

Located a mere twenty miles south, where barrier islands give way to mainland, a most comely and captivating beach dedicated solely to dog owners and their four-legged companions was nestled on a 500-foot stretch of beautiful white sand. The site itself is both shoreline and park, and is contained within chain-link fencing. Inside the perimeter, the County had installed a run for larger dogs and a separate area to accommodate smaller dogs. There was a shower area for rinsing sand and salt from their coats after they had spent the day frolicking. Advancing past the initial holding area and then negotiating yet another layer of gated containment, owners and their dogs make headway over a sand ridge that overlooks a wide expanse of beach, where dogs of all shapes and sizes are running free and swimming to their heart's content.

Now, one may think this kind of freedom could lead to fur-flying disaster in one form or another, but, I tell you—it is something about the Zen of the dog beach that places each and every dog in attendance into reposeful calm. All souls benefit from the lapping of the sea, the tickle of the sand. The canine soul is no different. There were at least 40 dogs on the dog beach that day, and there was not one snarl or snip, no dominance, no territorial marking; their souls just blissfully communed.

It was a splendid, late-spring day as we made our way south. It was just Pearl Bailey and me. The Professor was busy with end-of-semester duties, but I was anxious to explore. We arrived early afternoon and navigated our way through the park. Once we crested the sand ridge, I untethered Pearl Bailey's leash, but she didn't bolt at first. She just stilled and stared in great amazement. Then, after taking it all in, she darted off at Olympian speed headed for the crystalline waters of the Gulf. She swam, she sported, she made merry. It was as if she had awakened in Dog Disney World on her birthday, holding the winning lottery ticket. She darted to each beach blanket, making friends with both canines and owners as if she had known them her whole life. She was unplugged! I sighed audibly at the joy I was witnessing. Pearl Bailey was smiling. And moreover, she was smiling at me!

Chapter 28

Once acclimated, she would jaunt off to visit each blanket, making nice with person and pooch alike. She would return to my side, her tail ventilating like an oscillating fan, kissing me over and over again. Then she would dart off again toward the shore, getting involved in a game of Frisbee or stick-fetching, each time returning with kisses and affection for me. Only my sunglasses hid my tears of elation.

Exhausted and sated after the hours gave way to the setting sun, we reluctantly packed up and made the trek up the dune to the park area and showers. As we approached the sand ridge, Pearl Bailey looked back over her shoulder, and—I kid you not—she sighed. She looked up at me with the most beatific smile and just sighed.

chapter 29

Pearl Bailey's dreams were big the night we returned from Dog Beach—canine dreams that had her animated and murmuring sweet yips and yelps, and sugar-plum dreams that had her splashing, bobbing on a sea sparkling with diamonds. Those dreams would never awake her. They chased her right through until morning. Exhausted and spent from a day of undulating joy pulsing through her psyche, she rested and let the sweetness of her dreams fulfill her every notion.

I have to tell you: that night I sat and studied Miss Bailey as she slept. I squinted my eyes and surveyed her actions for an interpretation. And as funny as it sounds, as I watched, I began to soften. Not only was the day extraordinary in so many ways, it was a benevolent day, bringing about appreciation and recognition to both of our souls.

I told you that day was both a blessing and a curse, didn't I? The following morning, Pearl Bailey awoke at her normal time, shortly after sunrise. Being the overnight voyeur, I was slow to wake. Once I heard her rustling, I shook the cobwebs from my mind and began the process of rising. Pearl Bailey countered my every movement. She watched and waited as I made my way through the bathroom for morning toiletries. As we descended down the

Double Dealing Dog

stairs to grab a leash for our morning constitutional, Pearl Bailey was dancing. It was a kind of ridiculous prancing much better suited to a "foo-foo" dog than a canine of her size. Too early in the morning for antics, I tethered her up, and out we went, headed down the lane for our walk. Well, we didn't get past the SUV in the driveway when she put on the skids. If you ever heard the adage "You can't budge a big dog," then you get the picture. Here I was, at the bottom of the driveway, pulling on a canine like it was my job! Yet, to no avail. She would not move. We grappled and tussled with crossed swords until the sparring left me exhausted! Pearl Bailey was carefully positioned beside the passenger door, pinned with a hopeful heart. And I hadn't even had my coffee!

My calls for help shrieking out to The Professor had him in heart palpitations. As The Professor rounded the courtyard, don't you know that Miss Bailey hustled up her fanny and was all wags to The Professor? Of all the nerve! Professor took her leash from my hand, called her along and, of course, she listened up! Off they went, The Professor shaking his head in disbelief. Discombobulated at 7 a.m., I went off in search of my coffee and my wits.

chapter 30

Having made a truce, Pearl Bailey and I decided to take time at the beach together every day we could fit it in. It was clear that, if I took her to Dog Beach, she would behave, come when she was called, and not resist my commands–no nonsense. I was conditioning her to the point that, if she rebelled even so much as once, I would cancel the privilege. And so it was that a new routine would temper both our dispositions.

At first, we averaged only two days a week. We split it up—one morning visit and one afternoon visit. It wasn't long before we just began to follow the sun. If we woke and it was a bit overcast, we would wait for the afternoon. If we woke and the day was shining like a promise, we would head out after breakfast. The two days settled into a comfortable three days. Splitting the week was a very fair and even-handed balance. True to her stately countenance, Miss Pearl Bailey never once bent the rules. After our two-hour visit, she would walk with me up to the dune, and, always, she would turn and emit that "sigh," and then proceed with a hustle-up in her step and head off for the showers. Tomorrow is another day, Scarlett!

I was happy to continue this pattern as a matter of course. The forty-mile round trip drive didn't deter me. It seemed fair dues in

Double Dealing Dog

return for a dog that would mind her *P's & Q's!* Maybe our girl was maturing, after all. At nearly two years of age, Pearl Bailey hadn't slowed in her shenanigans at all. But these beach frolics seemed to temper the monkey business; after all, if your mother took you to the beach most every day and then, upon your return, released you to your own confines to chase lizards to your heart's content in a tropical Shangri-La, well, wouldn't *you* toe the line?

It was a shared agreement that we would keep the pace in providing the entertainment for Pearl Bailey, and she would reciprocate (for the most part) by flying right! I could live with that truce!

Chapter 30

chapter 31

As Miss Bailey matured, her initial captivating beauty blossomed into the most alluring and resplendent animal these eyes have ever seen. She was stunningly beautiful. Yet, true to her moniker, "The World's Worst Dog," Pearl Bailey, although tempered, still demonstrated countless other exasperating shenanigans on a regular basis.

One of her many charms—rolling in dirt. Miss Pearl Bailey, the color of a creamy, luminous pearl, delighted in a coat of muck and mire. This wasn't just puppy antics; she was now a full-fledged dog with a beautiful, long-feathered tail and underbelly! It was a daily ritual to her. The grimier she could get, the more glee in the heart! And, remember her penchant for hoses? In the Florida sunshine, plants need to be watered regularly. Now, Miss B found jubilation in the squirt of water as it percolated from the nozzle. She would jump and bite and twist her torso in all manner of distortion just to get to the stream! Then, when properly soaked to the gills, she would immediately roll about in the perfectly manicured mulch beds, packing her pelt with dirt and mud.

Here's another peccadillo, on a more personal note. Have you ever owned a favorite shirt or piece of clothing? I had what was classified as the "perfect" tee shirt. It was long-sleeved, soft, and comfortable. It fit like a dream and always looked good whether paired with jeans or dress-up. No matter what the day had in store for me, when I put on that shirt, everything turned my way. So you can imagine my ire the morning I reached for my shirt and, as I put it on, discovered that the sleeves on both arms had been uniformly chewed to ragged edges. Now, this was *both* arms and *both* in the *exact, same* spot. The meticulousness of Miss Bailey's signature destruction was beyond comprehension. The "how" and the "why" was left only to conundrum, because, try as I might, I could never figure her out!

Chapter 31

Here I will remind you that this dog *never*, not even *once*, demonstrated any type of this behavior in the presence of The Professor. Her exemplary conduct around him was beyond reproach.

chapter 32

Lady Ella Fitzgerald came into our life on a warm summer day during Miss Bailey's third year. Although I had never paused my quest in search of a companion for Pearl Bailey, nothing ever seemed to gel. I came close a couple of times, only to have disappointment descend upon my shoulders as I took the long count.

In the circle of my new island friends, I became most chummy with a beautiful soul who owned a Cairn Terrier. If you remember Toto in *The Wizard of Oz*, you are familiar with the breed. I reaped much amusement over my friend's terrier and, one day, this little spitfire stared me down with intent in her tawny chestnut eyes, as if to say, "My breed is a good choice." Well, now, being the professed Big Dog Girl, I was somewhat taken aback. I mean, a *terrier*? For me? That was something I never considered. Pondering the idea moved me to action, and, just like that, it seemed the deal was done!

Names are a big thing with me. Pearl Bailey came by her name in a quite fashionable way. First, let me be clear that she was named for the jazz great, Pearl Mae Bailey, whom I had the pleasure of meeting one night at a Georgetown jazz club in DC. But outside of that fact, the name settled well on Pearl Bailey, as she is the color of a pearl and was already named "Bailey" when The Professor purchased her. Now, all during my hunt for a canine companion for Miss Bailey, I had it in my mind that I would name her new sister "Ella," after the *First Lady of Song,* the legendary and most beloved jazz singer of all time, Ella Fitzgerald. What a tribute to the music genre I loved best!

I have always said that angels watch over me, but those in the know conclude it's more than that. The particular angels that are my guardians are hilarious and full of mirth. Having reached out to cyberspace late one night, I tripped upon a breeder of Cairns that was geographically desirable. In a flurry, I typed off a hasty message to the breeder recounting my lament on wanting to add a companion to our family. It was in taking this action that I received a call the very next morning! It was the breeder with an interesting proposition. He had sold a pair of Cairn sisters to a family down south a few months before, and the professional couple had just alerted him that they were being transferred back to the *Big Apple* for work. As painful as it was, the family would not be able to take the girls with them. And so it was that the breeder was heading down to meet this couple to take the girls back to the breeding farm in order to re-home them to a new family. He inquired if I would be interested in one of the puppies. Well, "Sure," I said, "I will take a look."

Following my instinct, I set off that same day to meet the breeder as he made his way back north with the little girls. As clandestine as it seems, we met at a rest area off of Interstate 75. The gentleman breeder had the two girls corralled in a playpen and all were sitting at a picnic bench, patiently waiting my arrival. As I approached, I was wholly captivated by the cuteness factor of these two little balls of fur! They were playful and enchanting—both of them. I took turns picking them up, playing with them, and, although they were

Chapter 32

both attentive, the one that stole my heart immediately was the one who looked straight into my eyes with endearing, adoring love. Instinctively, I knew. I cleared my throat and asked the breeder if this little one had a name? He replied, "Ella." Boy, but the heavenly hosts were chuckling down at me!

chapter 33

From the onset, Pearl Bailey and Lady Ella became the best of friends, and it was all I had hoped for. Our household was once again a theatre for two canine souls full of boisterous fun. I hadn't known this kind of double-trouble since my sheepdog pair, Ulysses and Chelsea Beatrice, who would cavort through the house non-stop. The unfortunate part was that our Miss Bailey was secretly teaching her cohort, the eight-pound "Lil Scamp," all of her bad habits. The first thing Lady Ella figured out was that it was possible not to come when you are called. "Ignore all humans—they don't really mean it when they call you"—always an attractive trait in a canine companion. The other incensing trait that our little Lady Ella had embraced was lizard-chasing. Now, of course, true to the instincts of her breed, a terrier makes a fine huntress. These two Mutt-and-Jeff characters fed off of each other's energy in the pursuit of the Holy Grail—the billions of Florida's geckos! Where Pearl Bailey was a stalker, Lady Ella was a digger and a barker. Our new addition made it clear vocally that she would reign over any reptile brave enough to stand its ground! And, if it scooted behind a plant or flower, it would be dug up in the most frenzied fashion. Realizing there was nothing I could do about this deeply imbedded instinct, I joined in the merriment

Double Dealing Dog

and called out to them to come a-runnin' when I witnessed any lizard activity on the deck!

Pearl Bailey had literally developed jaws of steel. Her biting strength and speed in the *pousuite de lézards* was honed by the crushing of soda cans. Yes, just like a mangy old goat, PB was a chewer of cans! How horrifying it is to see your beautiful, expensive, and gorgeous retriever attempt to eat the V-8 can you just finished drinking! You know that can't be good for her. Ugh! And mind you, that reptile prey she may be stalking? Don't forget, she's going to devour it as well!

It is a wondrous sight to watch canine souls commune. The instinct to form a pack is so clearly apparent. Pearl Bailey did become, as I had hoped, somewhat of a mother dog. She was sweet and docile, but rough and tumble, letting Lady Ella rise to any challenge. Their independent personalities somehow melded into sweet dependence on each other. And when that happened, I no longer worried about the ever-exasperating Pearl Bailey. I just joined their pack, and that was a great start. Yes, it was us three girls. Girls! This was new to me. I had lived with all that testosterone when it was just me, The Professor, and our two boys. Now *girl-power* was instilled in our household, and it was a glorious feeling. Finding unity and becoming part of a united front made the past indiscretions of Pearl Bailey drift away to a faded memory. In some respects, Lady Ella's *monkey business* became more of an immediate concern than that of Miss Bailey, but only to a miniature degree! Now, I am not saying that the devilish retriever leader of the pack was no longer exasperating—she was! It's the change in *me* in refereeing their antics that was profound. I melded into the pack, and therefore, adapted and followed the path of their canine souls. Although it was a gradual transformation for me, it was one that resulted in tremendous resolve.

chapter 34

Change was in the air in more ways than one. The Florida summer rains gave away to warm days and cool nights that are so perfectly alluring. My writings were expanding, and the prose that resulted was notable. The rhythm of the days cross-faded into the sweetness of the evenings. My heart became more appreciative, and the expressive style of my narrative reached greater depths. This syncopated growth brought about a sense of gentility that softened my newfound perspective. Although still an excavator at heart, and, intent on rolling in the resultant mound of dirt, Pearl Bailey responded to this global change in me. No longer was I her mere foil, so Pearl Bailey sought out other mischievous amusements, albeit less menacing, and, I, in turn, reciprocated with renewed vitality in remaining devoted to her.

Having adopted a somewhat learned behavior, Little Ella grew quickly and became the new instigator in all matters of rabble-rousing. However, channeling her energy was as easy as whisking up her twelve-pound frame with one hand!

A newfound peace and repose permeated my persona, and the effect trickled down to the canine souls resting at my feet.

It's odd. Whenever change descends upon one's essence, a quietude always seems to follow to complete the process.

Double Dealing Dog

chapter 35

I'd like to state for the record that life has treated me more than well. I have been fortunate to have imparted and accepted love and devotion. My canine companions have been constant throughout every step of my journey from childhood to my aging, itchy but achy bones. It was particularly the profound love from animal souls that allowed me to grow, to heal, to amplify and cultivate my belief that there is, central within every living being, a pure pearl of goodness.

Most who know me will agree that I'm not a religious being, but I *am* a deeply spiritual one. I've trekked, studied, and made inquiries into all divine doctrine before landing on the one belief to which I adhere. This credo is based on one of the oldest religions, its unchanging axiom having survived these many thousands of years. A major tenet of my conviction has been formed by the undeniably peaceful aspects of ancient Eastern religions.

My beloved father, with his open intelligence and worldly knowledge, allowed me the freedom to formulate my own view. And that is exactly what I did. I carried these words with me, "Daughter, I do not care what faith you embrace, as long as you always keep it constant in your life." These words delivered me to a place where I learned to quench my soul by feeding the souls of others with love, kindness, and compassion, a place wherein the beauty of music, the unwavering love from a canine, and the need to serve as caretaker fashioned me into the woman I am today. I am keenly aware that, without the profound and unconditional love that one receives from the canine spirit, I could not willingly succeed. It tempers me.

Pearl Bailey, while easily winning the award of being "the most exasperating of all the canine spirits who have walked beside me," has in her own way metaphysically transported me to a place of tolerance and co-existence. Our respective natures, while diametrically opposed, found a way not only to coexist but to flourish, even within the dependence of her pack. That, in itself, is the most incisive precept that has shaped my life, my soul, and my spirit.

I know unequivocally that as long as I walk this green Earth, I will walk with at least one canine soul beside me. The best dog or the world's worst, both of our souls will thrive and survive because we have each other.

Chapter 35

I have heard it said that. . . .

Good souls give you happiness,

Bad ones give you experience,

The worst ones give you lessons,

And the best ones give you memories!

Dedicated to Samuel, one of the great ones!

acknowledgments

There are challenges in writing a novel that is somewhat based on a true story. The characters, naturally borrowed from one's own experience, are sometimes easily recognized by type. Their collective animation in print, however, is difficult to camouflage. All the characters live within me. Otherwise, I could not possibly give them life.

So, and in no particular order, my eternal gratitude goes to my editor, Danny Ray, for his insightful, keen, and generous mind. Danny, not only have you have taught me how to expand my voice, both musically and through composition, you have single-handedly made me a better writer.

And, I send a special thank-you/shout-out to my sister, Kelly Ann, together with her family. Their combined and endless antics and escapades have continually motivated me to create. In our upbringing, Sister Golden Hair, we share a very rich and precious heritage. Aren't we fortunate?

Many thanks to my "daughter," Brooke, for leading me through one loss and onto another love, that of Big Max, and who gave me the beautiful-faced Baby Beckett, who inspires me every single day.

Thanks to my daughter-in-law, Lori, whose stories supplied me the lowdown on contemporary student life and who also gave me the singing, dancing, back-flipping Madilyn Isabella, a great inspiration all her own!

Of special note—many thanks to Kathleen "Bella," who spent the final days of this book with me nestled in the flagship of modern American literary triumph: New York's Algonquin Hotel. Kathleen, you absolutely infuse every day with such gaiety. It is impossible not to be buoyant in your presence!

And finally, on the home front, no book would ever get completed if not for the love, devotion, and absolute, unconditional love of my husband, Ron. You're a rock star! Let's keep it going so we can develop a sequel!

about the author

d.j. posner is a native of Washington, DC, and now resides on Siesta Key, Florida along with her husband and two canine muses. Her prescription for living with a joy-filled, positive and generous spirit has carried her through life's many challenges. Through her writing, she shares this ideology with her readers so they may seek and claim that feeling for themselves.

www.ingramcontent.com/pod-product-compliance
Lightning Source LLC
Chambersburg PA
CBHW042117100526
44587CB00025B/4084